# MORNING



Good morning!

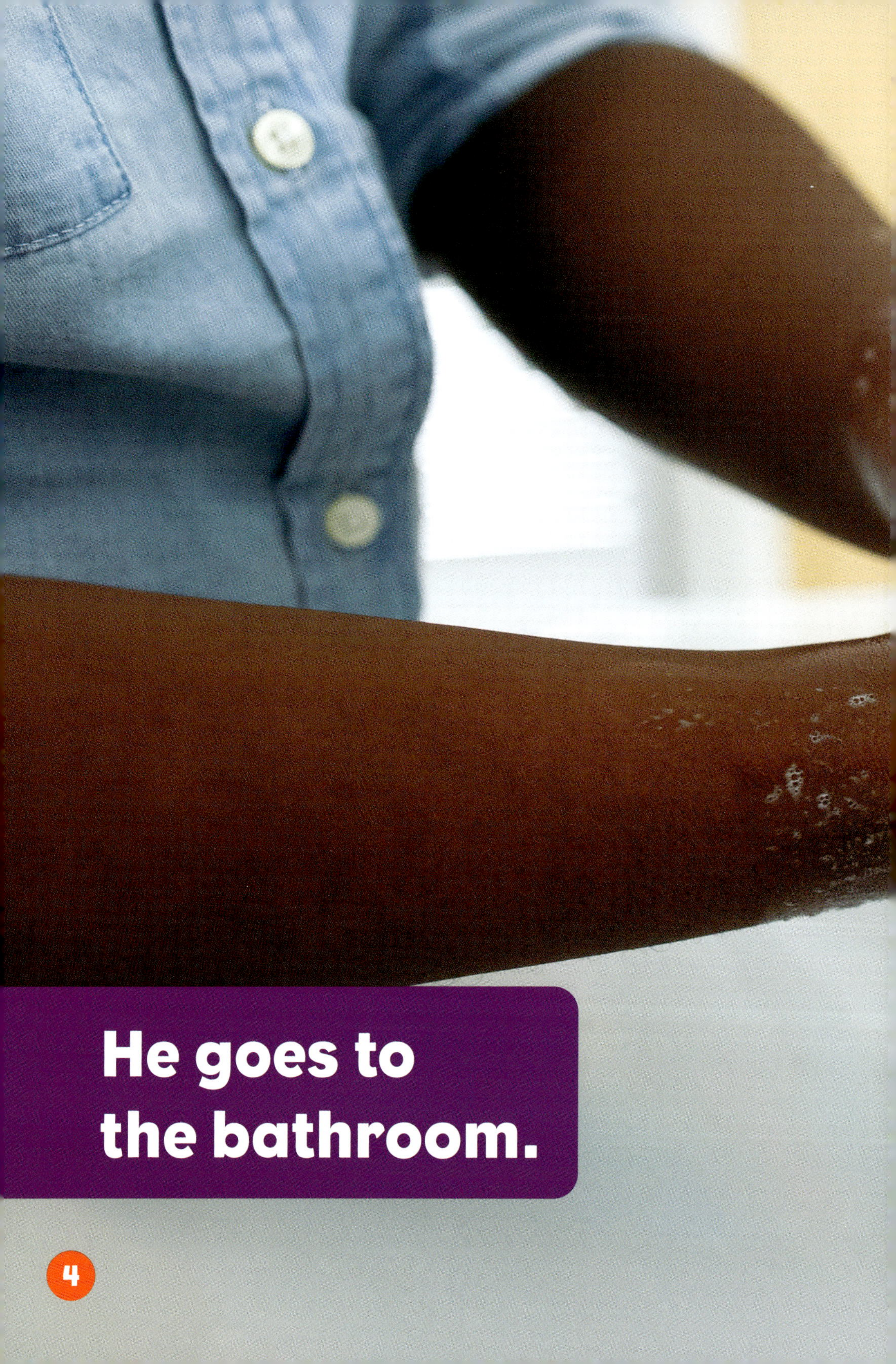

He goes to the bathroom.

He washes his hands.

brush

She brushes her hair.

He brushes his teeth.

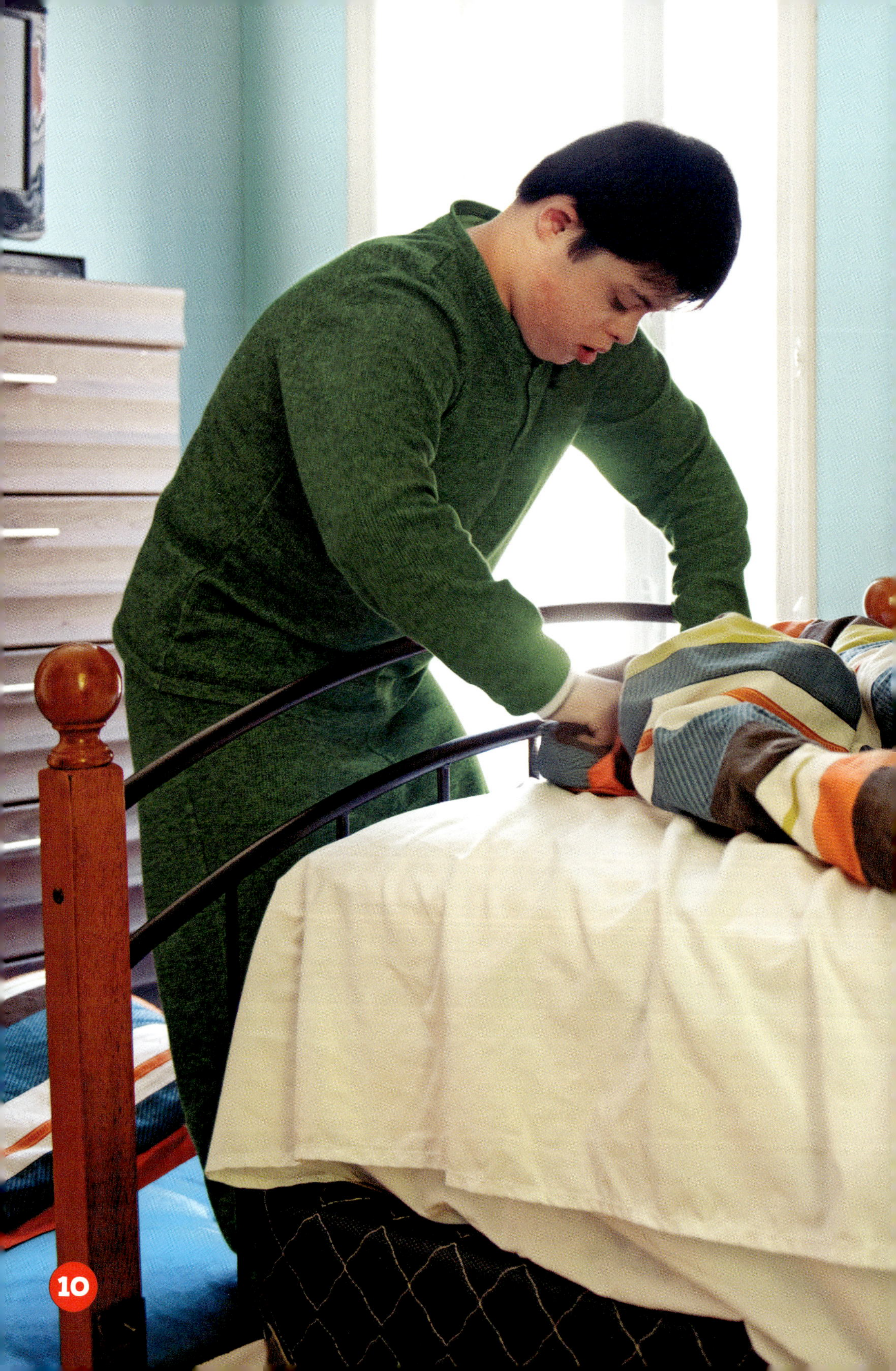

He makes his bed.

We eat breakfast.

EMERGENCY EXIT

We are ready for school!

# LET'S REVIEW!

**Which action below is not part of the morning routine in the book?**

# INDEX